HIDDEN RIVER

Stephanie Norgate was born and grew up in Selborne. Playing in Gilbert White's house and garden impelled an early love of nature and of writing. She now lives in West Sussex with her husband, writer Stephen Mollett, and their two children. She read English and Latin literature at the universities of Warwick and Oxford. She has worked on a kibbutz, as a waitress, barmaid, beach shop assistant, apple picker, temp, in a concrete factory, as a bookseller, a teacher, an Arvon Foundation Centre Director and university lecturer.

Her first radio play, *The Greatest Gift*, won a *Radio Times* Drama Award in 1988. Other radio plays include *Clive* (1998), the story of a fostered teenager, and *The Journalistic Adventures of an American Girl in London* (Woman's Hour Serial, 2003) which dramatised the life of Elizabeth L. Banks, one of the first undercover female reporters in Victorian London. Her stage plays have been performed and read on the London and Edinburgh Fringe (Old Red Lion, Lyric Studio, Hammersmith, Celtic Lodge) and include *Naked in the Garden*, based on the life of Artemisia Gentileschi (Finborough Theatre).

Her pamphlet collection, *Fireclay* (Smith/Doorstop, 1999), was a Poetry Business competition winner in 1998. A generous selection of poems appeared in *Oxford Poets 2000* (Oxford Carcanet, 2000). She received an Arts Council Writer's Award for her poetry in 2002. Her translated versions of poetry have appeared in *Modern Poetry in Translation*. Recent poetry commissions include riddles and stories to accompany the Alfred the Great exhibition in 2008. She teaches at the University of Chichester, where she runs the MA in Creative Writing.

Hidden River (Bloodaxe Books, 2008) is her first full-length collection.

STEPHANIE NORGATE

Hidden River

BLOODAXE BOOKS

ISBN: 978 1 85224 796 6

First published 2008 by
Bloodaxe Books Ltd,
Highgreen,
Tarset,
Northumberland NE48 1RP.

www.bloodaxebooks.com
For further information about Bloodaxe titles
please visit our website or write to
the above address for a catalogue.

Bloodaxe Books Ltd acknowledges
the financial assistance of
Arts Council England, North East.

Cover design: Neil Astley & Pamela Robertson-Pearce.

Printed in Great Britain by
Bell & Bain Limited, Glasgow, Scotland.

for Stephen

ACKNOWLEDGEMENTS

Acknowledgements are due to the editors of the following publications in which some of these poems first appeared: *The Arvon Journal*, *Dreaming Beasts* (Krebs & Snopes, 2003), *The Forward Book of Poetry 2000*, *Forward Poems of the Decade*, *Magma*, *Modern Poetry in Translation*, *Mouth Ogres* (Oxmarket, 2001), *Mslexia*, *The North*, *Op Het Lijf Gedragen* (Protestantse Pers, 2005), *Oxford Poetry*, *Oxford Poets 2000* (Oxford Carcanet, 2000), *The Poetry Cure* (Bloodaxe Books/Newcastle University, 2005), *Poetry London*, *Reactions 3: New Poetry* (pen&inc, 2002), and *Writing Women*.

Several of these poems were published in *Fireclay* (Smith/Doorstop, 1999), a winner of The Poetry Business pamphlet competition.

'Sussex Road at Night in December' was recorded on a Tongues and Strings CD. 'Green Lane' was a postcard poem commissioned by Arts Council England, Museum Libraries Archives South East and the Society of Chief Librarians to celebrate National Poetry Day and to encourage reading.

I am indebted to Arts Council England for a writer's award in 2002.

Thanks also to my friends, colleagues and students (past and present) at the University of Chichester for the inspiring environment, for time taken and given, most particularly Kate Betts, Isla Duncan, Hugh Dunkerley, Alison MacLeod, Maggie Sawkins, Karen Stevens and David Swann.

Many thanks to Helen Dunmore and Bernard O'Donoghue for reading individual poems, and to Vicki Feaver for reading the whole manuscript.

Some poems are dedicated to the memory of my parents, Myrtle and Charles Norgate. Finally, my best thanks and love to Stephen and to our children, Francesca and Ben.

CONTENTS

Mud Bath

Sitting down in mud,
we pack it tight on skin,
delicately finger it under eyes,
massage it into breasts and inside thighs,
shape each other's backs,
as if sculpting mud onto a frame. Now we are
wild women, wild men, the first people of the early world,
made from earth and water to stare at the sky,
our feet growing from the ground.

When we stand, the gaps we leave
fill like quicksand
as if we've taken nothing from the earth.

Our eyes peer through holes in mud-masks,
as we lean in the sun, statues drying,
the thick wet glaze turning to plaster.
Then we come alive, and, cracking as we move,
slide into sulphurous water,
let our feet drift, see our moulds
loosen, lift, dissolve,
grey clouds swirling in the hot spring.

We dry out on beach mats,
watch alligators, in the farm next door,
open jaws, slowly snap, sink into mud,
only their eyes visible through the barrier,
watching us, now we are flesh again.

The Wheedling Man

Just because he spoke in a wheedling sort of way,
just because he looked ashamed and afraid,
just because he whined and crouched,
just because he was so aware of his lost life,
fingering the old bus-pass in his pocket,
the photograph of his wife, just because
he drew his jacket round him against the cold
even though it was a warm blue day,
just because he puckered his face and looked like he might cry,
or suddenly piss on the venerable paving-stones,
just because he wouldn't let up, was desperate
and sad, I didn't give him anything.
And now it's no consolation
to the hungry wheedling man, that he's stayed in my head
and won't go away, that I can replay every word of what he said,
how he looked; that I'm still walking down the lovely old alleyway
with its famous trace of an open sewer,
swishing my feet in gold-fingered horsechestnut leaves,
thinking of this man I meet everyday at four for sex,
(but not so crudely as that, in a kind of haze)
when he gets up from under the wall and approaches me,
his voice whining in my ear, his tweedy jacket
brushing my shoulder,
please love love please love spare me some change
dancing in front of me, stopping me getting on.
But two hours earlier, a man
with matted hair and Rasputin eyes
said to me firmly, 'I need two pounds. Give it me.'
And I gave instantly.

Echo

They say she's a late talker, haunting the garden,
digging mud-ovens to cook weeds.

Alone, sun lighting up closed curtains,
she'll jab her fingers into bowls of silver ash,
as if the glitter dust she dabs on hands and arms
will make her visible.

When there is a space in the air for the word to fit
among the jigsaw pieces of other people's speech,
when she feels the word's first stirring in her mouth,
aware of its shape, the breath it takes, then she starts
her tongue moving, saying it once, saying it once more,
and with every word, an echo.
      Did she say it?
Did she hear herself say it?
      She looks in mirrors
to see her own mouth move. She looks in mirrors
mouthing at herself, like Narcissus, the way
he loved his own reflection. And she's both
Narcissus and Echo, calling shun, shun,
reflect, shun, fleck, shun, reflection,
checking the mirror to see if she's still there
whispering each phrase again, loving, *loving*
to see her voice clothe itself in bones and skin, *skin*,
to see the whispers misting the glass,
and the shape on the surface where her lips pressed
showing, before it fades, a ripple, a *kiss*.

Photos of Kosovo

and I thought how through it all
someone was growing dahlias

storing tubers in boxes all winter
cutting roots to grow rows and rows

of deep red cactus dahlias
protecting shoots from frost

and someone was growing roses
feeding them with blood and bone,

and someone was buying them
from a cold lorry packed with buds

perhaps juggernauts of flowers were crossing
Europe, their drivers gassing at service stations

their hands chilled by damp stems
bags of carnations piled high

they don't unwrap them
photos of photos pinned to wooden stakes

bags of deep red dahlias
their cellophane crackling

like the papers I rifle through
for the quiet village murders we hardly notice now

if it wasn't for you
in a helicopter with Rich beside you

his head swivelling like an eagle-owl's
I'd probably be reading about the prince's mistress

how the mind refuses to settle on bags of bodies
grown row after row *they don't unwrap them*

and follows instead the journeying friend,
the trading of flowers

Tupperware

That summer all the women were wild for tupperware
and held parties to sell pale plastic and opaque lids.
There were tinned salmon sandwiches and sausages on sticks
and cress the kids had grown on flannels. Permed and perfumed
they danced to James Last's *Tijuana Brass*, their eyes Latin and intense,
their homemade dresses flaring round their legs. *See, it seals*, they said,
it seals, keeping everything fresh, wasting nothing. So they kept
the jugs, the bowls, the cake containers. The children, up late, laughing
through the door's crack, knew nothing of big stale larders,
brown jugs standing in bowls of water, butter on a cool cleft shelf
in a deep cottage wall, raw meat on a square slab of marble,
or of girls who'd been hungry and cycled everywhere, who knew how to use
each cabbage leaf, each dreg of milk or lump of dough. Later
the women would snap shut a single sausage or a spoonful of jelly
and pile the leftovers, box after box, into their singing refrigerators.

'A perfect example of a paralysed larynx'

In the waiting-room we'd stared
for hours at the umbrella pine
in a painting someone had put there
to help us wait. The sky leaked
over the moor, the moor leaked its heather
over the frame, the purple light leaked
into the wall from the open field
while your ballooning arm
leaked into the chair.

The consultant's voice was clean
and quick. 'May I take your photograph?'
His students, busy cartographers,
gathered up their implements,
torches, lenses, clipboards,
words like 'block of disease'.
And there was your chest,
pale as a birch and as thin,
the blue islands, blue as pines,
like a map some pressure of geography
had caused. 'Of course,'
you said, glad to be useful again.

'Come here and look at this
perfect example of a paralysed larynx.'

Yet you could still speak
and to me your voice sounded
no different, textured, lyrical
like a rough piece of wood you'd handle
and plane or turn into shape,
forests in that voice,
beech and larch and teak,
a good bit of oak,
some pine grained as streaming water,
as wood shavings scattered on a sawdust floor.

Months later, driving through woods
there's a patch of larches, made
papery and apricot by light,
their evergreen shapes at odds
with their orange needled leaves,
and something of you has leaked

into them, something you would
have said about larchwood, some lost
knowledge, some connection only
I can make now with the saw's rasp
or planks lined up how you wanted them
or with a student in the hospital, holding
the photograph and peering
like a craftsman at the blue islands
of your chest. In the ark of suffering
maybe you are there with him,
handing him the tools, advising,
that long muscle of your voice,
unbotched and clear.

Water on the Moon

My father says, 'They've found water
on the moon.' Sheets and frozen depths of it.
We're going up.
The lift walls are as pitted as a cratered surface,
as shiny metallic as a child's silver-foil crescent,
pressed with creases.

They have found ice
                    hidden in the wells of the moon.
Galileo's dark seas are solid pools
                    clamped under the rocks of the moon.
They know what to do with moon-ice, how to mine it,
                    melt it into breath and fuel.
Visitors to the moon will return under their own steam.

When the doors open
we hear of water and blood hiding
in the kelpy spaces of my mother's lung.
There's an ebb and flow in her chest, a secret sea.

Returning late,
I see the moon, misty and waterlogged,
lighting my way past the night-closed crocuses,
past the myrtle bush spiked by fierce peppery leaves,
and the myrtle is as dark and as mediterranean in the watered light
as my mother's eyes, growing larger
with every sigh of her secret sea.

Early Morning

I'm watching a lizard at the window's mesh,
shocked to stillness by the fan's turning,

which whirrs me to hospital nights, and you dying.
You dying reminds me to live in this moment

of roofs hanging on hilltop air, white and wall-less,
brushstrokes of cypress marking the mist,

the bell in the tower at Pancole floating,
about to fly off, if it weren't roped to earth.

Maybe you came here in war time, despatch rider,
grinding up these sharp curves to the farm.

Maybe you mouthed words of pigeon Italian,
pictured some welcome of grappa or wounds.

There you are, dismounting so quickly,
resting the bike you've ridden through mines.

Now we're both standing at the farm's gateway,
drenched in low cloud, dampened by grass.

We're craning our heads to see into the future.
I know that you'll live. You know nothing of me.

The gun leaves its holster. You walk to the threshold.
I'm willing you on to a kindly reception:

perhaps a young woman runs forward with coffee,
perhaps an old man offers you bread.

The door closes slowly. There's a gap on the gravel.
The lizard unfreezes, flits off, thought igniting.

The bell clangs, unveils long rows in the vineyard.
Heat burns vapour, returns the ground to my feet.

Leave, 1945

'You mean you haven't told them?' said a lady
on the bus. Already he could feel
the quick distrust. 'They've moved, you know.'
To a cottage where he'd have to make a ceiling,
fix the windows, build new stairs. He had
to stop himself from walking out beyond
the village, up the tunnelled lane
to the old house, growing lonely on the hill.

He beat a swift tattoo on the front door,
had to wait a moment before he saw
her face fall for the cake she hadn't made,
the floor that wasn't swept, for the crumbling
plaster in the hall. 'You didn't tell us,'
was all she said. The new house was much older,
soft and low. He tried not to let his eyes
show how the new house suited them.
The bedroom was too cramped.
He pulled his mattress out
on meadow grass, and only then, face
up to the stars, did he smell the trees, feel
on his skin all the miles of Africa
and Italy he'd travelled to come home.

Lamping

It's as if a drunk's careering
down the slope,
blasting rifles,
aiming searchlights
along dark thin combs of grass.

I've seen rabbits
walleyed, strange, a blueness round their lids,
and feared their weakness,
the gummy trickles on their fur.

So this is better:
the lamps blaze and turn, like wrecker's lights.

I want to scream a warning –
the splintering of small bones, lead in the lungs.

Huge haloes catch the rabbits in their sun.

In the morning, the rooks
I love and look for everyday
are vulture swaying shadows on the field.

Survivors feed
on scored, criss-crosses of grass
unseeded by the tearing wheels.

Light Trap

He's tried hanging a lamp over a white sheet,
or, when he was younger,

lining a cardboard box with baco-foil
and stuffing a lead through it,

screwing on the hundred-watt bulb.
Now he uses ultraviolet in a drum,

fitting a perspex collar with vanes,
funnelling them to the centre,

and, mindful of panic,
he cuts refuges, twigs of sycamore,

alder, oak. He likes to watch
the procession of shivering wings,

ghosts, hawks, burnets, loopers, browns,
drawn to the beam,

streaming down the clouded night.
In the morning, he frees them,

slivers of bark shaken from bark,
while he imagines for a moment

the long tubular heart,
the double nerve-cord,

the assaulting sweetness of nectar,
pheromones, the swift muscular beat.

Green Lane

Though you've cut me with lay-bys and ring roads,
where once droves of cattle pounded my back,
though you think I'm silenced, my voice still churrs
from sheltering hedges. I knot my roots into yours.
I'm your ditch of sandstone, your mess of goosegrass,
unreeling over downs, a gap in the may.
Come into me now when rain falls on a green morning.
I won't trickle away, dead end to a building site.
No, I'll hang a gate between the forest and mist.
You'll lift the latch, walk me, through gorse, to the sea.

John Clare's Shoes

She invites me in. There are no doors;
each frame's become a hole.
There's the sigh of a thin curtain,

but walls have ears.
All night my pubic bone aches.
The waters build in me like seas.

I hear bodies slither in a bag,
couples coming breast to breast,
the child's early dawning words.

I stroke the stacked doors,
wishing I could lift
each hard oak-panel, stop the gaps.

It's day in the museum, but I'm haunted
by the intimacies of night, as if the house
had a thousand mouths, which would talk, talk, talk.

And then I see Clare's shoes
in their glass coffin, unlaced,
black leather sides sagging, heels downtrod.

His shoes have battered tongues,
worn soles that tramped
through sunken lanes of seeding grass, vamping

out of doors with heavy locks,
away from rooms
which babbled like gods.

Three Definitions of Volume

We can find no scar,
But internal difference
Where the Meanings are
    EMILY DICKINSON

A big white cracked rectangle, *sink*,
sopping ribbed sleeves and happiness –
that you could fit this into this into this
filling dented aluminium jugs with water
slopping one into the other or eight into one
gripping the black bakelite handles:
eighth (toy size), quarter pint,
a half-pint, a pint, quart, gallon
lining up the jugs like Russian dolls
teetering in order on the porcelain edge.
You might have been five, six, seven
less than half the mass you are now, and a sixth of your age
inside the same body.
With one sip
(from a wine glass, a cup, a mug,
the miracle of unchanging volume changing shape)
you replay
        the word VOL on a red plastic knob
and the hand that wouldn't or couldn't
turn it down and the throat that couldn't
stop screaming, the sound echoing all day

through David Copperfield, blue buckram with gold inlay,
faded copperplate inscription, pressed spider in the centre,
torn spine, mildewed paper which smells of sick,
through Jane Eyre, second-hand,
fat octavo, red pasteboard, tiny print,
a woman in flames crying for water
which gushes from the tap while the jugs clink,
the children chatter and slide on the wet floor;
and you're wondering whether you really saw
the sun in the water and ladled it right up
into the gallon jug in a rippling skein
of shining cold reflection.

Breeding

Last season, I bought a dog
for my muff, bred to tiny bones,
with a grey, silky coat.

My hands grew warm
on its heartbeat and blood,
as the carriage went visiting

over the frozen river.
Copycats on smaller allowances
longed for body heat too

and drugged the farmer's ferrets
to lie snoozing in the dark
tunnels of their muffs.

I laughed at them, explaining
that one could train a dog
so easily with a sweetmeat

from the New Year's table,
though the whimperings,
damp patches and wriggling

made for the occasional gaucherie,
and once there was that stench of blood.
Yes, though it was a legendary winter,

I suffered no chilblains on my fingers
only the occasional nip,
or flea bite, which barely showed.

True, there was a risk of stepping
on it in my long yellow skirts
when the muff dog went wild

and worried my petticoats to death.
This season, there's no need to bother cook
about its diet of mashed liver.

These new handwarmers,
tins of hot charcoal in red velvet bags,
are much more efficacious.

Metro Boy

Maybe that's his father with a polystyrene cup
up under the nose of a commuter who averts her eyes,
sighs and mouths above the violin, 'He should be in school.'
'Fool. Fuck you. This boy knows already how to play.'

Aged five or younger, Wolfgang could compose in different keys.
Trees shivered off their snow. Salzburg echoed to his chords.
Swords clattered to the floor. Wooden tops unwound.
Sound was every new thing. Leopold praised and raged.

Sleeping in a trailer, out of town, by the maize field,
steeled by tracks, this boy dreams in minims, quavers,
savours the black leaping notes that climb the bars.
Cars murmur nursery rhythms in his head, keeping

time with some vague remembered fingering. 'Bitch,
bitch,' his stepfather shouts out to the night's halved moon.
Soon a requiem slowdances its way into the boy's mind,
winds the opening of train doors into the ostinato's rhyme.

Don Giovanni's Puppeteer

What they don't see:
the pulling on of opaque black legs,
the long-sleeved leotard,
my coarse fair hair flattened with spray,
the black hood drawn skull tight.

Luis advising me, his breath in my ear.

Mothballs, patchouli oil,
white dust in the velvet cloak,
the skin of all the actors
for the past hundred years.

I begin at the feet
sliding mine in, become his soles.
I fasten the anklets tight,
buckle our belts at the waist,
wear a loose canvas noose
about my neck, clip it neatly to his collar.
When I've slipped my hands in his,
Luis binds our wrists.

They choose not to see
how I've become his bones,
his dancing spine, a tree
of bloodbranches he can hang on,
how I can twitch his pelvis,
or jerk him down to hell.

And when they've clapped and gone,
and he's untied us, Luis talks to him,
retouches his papered face with paint,
mends the tiny gathered stitches in his breeches.

I strip, graze my knees
in the shallow littered pool,
hear the evening liners coming in,
watch tram lights ripple, magnify
blue tiles; I open and close
my own legs, letting the daywarmed water in,
thinking of what they don't dream, will never see,
Luis, this morning early,

saying he wants me standing,
turning my face to the wall,
lifting my arms from my side,
fumbling for my heart.

On Clothes Lines

Between two dug-in beams, my neighbour's line is a bowstring, tautened
by a metal pole.
Wooden pegs –
upside down sparrows – apostrophise the sky.

In Venice, they've rigged lines over fondamente and canals,
with pulleys to haul in catches of red shirts, skirts, table linen
;in the vaporetto's wake, lines of colour ripple.
On voting nights in Lisbon, flags rustle from lines
;slogans sag on narrow streets, zig-zag over balconies.
In Gulval, they've tied lines to masts, which clink as if they've never left their boats
;sheets are sails that want to float these terraces out of their dry dock.

Lucretius, watching clothes flapping by the sea, found proof of atomism.
So – he had a line.

The line's leap

: a turquoise shirt tugging at the day
;children ghosting through a tunnel of sheets
;windsocks of arms and legs, fighting the yard.

And after

:the scent on you – whether it's of lilac, the smoke of an exhausted fire, diesel,
spice from the Thai café, the mizzle – down here in the subway,
on your journey to work, you still wear the airing on your skin.

Some lineage. My mother's hands pegging laundry.
The artistry of hanging
:a harnessing of space and shape, fitted to a line.
The instruments
:pegs, sea-bleached as plastic jetsam.
Some lineage. My father's hands carving a groove in a batten, making
a prop for the line, an upturned diviner's rod,
tremoring at clouds.

These are the risks
:big drops on your hair, panic to unpeg and pile the wash
– its dark stain spreading in a drumming shower –
back into the basket.

If, slatternly, you leave out washing over night or over days, moths
camouflage themselves in folds
                    ;holes fray.
A cricket may hop on a sleeve,
                    fidget into a crease, spring out when you shake out the shirt,
                    hide under your bed, wings singing.
The evidence of birds
                            :white splashes or ditchings of elderberry.

                    Acid rain will scar, permeate.

        Frost
:a sheet, starched by a minus degree, stiffens to a square of cold, hard to unfold.
Some fading
                :put clothes out in a heat wave at noon to insolate, to apricate
        (for their drying is like the pleasure of words and as free),
                            and the black will weather
to an earth tone, the red to a dusted rose.

                    All summer, we dodge the washing in town squares
;we could steal a household's worth of clothes hung out in the common air
:

Umbra

The café's gold umbrellas,
rippling the morning sea,
call me to take cover
under the makeshift roof,
where the shadow of a friend,
who drew away from light,
sits with me, drinking an espresso,
fingers curved on the handle
of the small white cup,
the other hand fooling
with a glass of iced water,
until the sun dawdles on,
and when I look again,
my companion's gone
and those half empty cups
and glasses on the tin table
could belong to anyone.

The Umbrella

(after Weldon Kees and Mary Fedden)

Dear Weldon,
I've found the umbrella you mention,
shot out, the black silk stripped
to a few tatters. It looks shocked,
like a man who has seen too much.

The slender ribs are
lodged in an oak,
whose canopy casts shade
on a field of clocks,
clouds on milky sticks.

A breeze shifts the seeds.
Up they float,
spiky transparent parasols,
spreading their kind.

Perhaps the torn fabric
spawned threads,
stray rags, which float over
the sea, grow into forests
or mushrooms.
As for the empires you cite,
the umbrella would gladly
be free of them,
resting its struts
in the tree's shade until
the storm starts up again
and rips its remains
back into the fray.

The Night Square

Skateboarders angle against steps,
            demonstrate friction, force,
a child's physics.
            The square demands of them
the bump, the jolt, the jump,
            and more – to be shape changers.
Two feet merge, a thin flipper,
            or wing, a diver's spring to air.
One long skid.
            Their night rolls forwards.

Where am I in this?
            An obstacle they skim round.
In the dark of our flat, they are crashing weights,
            slicing the air,
throwing the loud voice
            that pretends it's me,
that has fixed itself like a board on my mouth,
            tripping my tongue
till I'm upside down, face skating the ground.

The battered square amplifies
            the rattle of crates, women shouting,
motorbike air,
            wheels on its paved runway, judderings.
When I think about landings,
            no images come.
Only the night's percussion echoes
            through humidity.

In the morning, pools of beer show sky.
            Jags of green glass
draw sun to the square's dense stone.
            Refractions survive brokenness.
A boy unreels a path across paving,
            unrolls our street behind him:
the day's experiment –

The Bones

(for Claire Halpin)

I'd suddenly driven back to the old flat,
missing you. And there you were washing bones

in a bucket and laying the washed bones
to dry on a big soft towel on your bed.

You were back and forth to the bath
emptying the sandy muddied water from the bones,

coding the bones carefully,
packing a tower of boxes with numbered bones.

From under the peeling bathroom of the flat,
I could smell lemongrass, satay, peanut oil, beef.

When we went down to eat,
our words breathing lime and gin,

the bones were dancing in our eyes.
We were listening to the hunger

of skeletons you'd found in a field
all planted round with antlers and gold,

listening to them jigging above us in their boxes,
listening to our bones answer.

Haiku from Lucretius

I *Aulis*

More often religion, rather than reason, gives birth to violence.
(DRN BOOK 1 *ll.* 80-101)

Mem, I fear your fear –
that embarking on reason
is somehow sinful.

But think of Aulis –
how the Greeks spilt a girl's blood.
Iphianassa

dressed for a wedding,
ribbons hanging from her hair,
trembled up the aisle

to meet her father.
The minister hid the sword.
The crowd was crying.

She fell on her knees,
silenced by fear, was hauled
forward by his men.

No husband. No hymns.
No peal of bells. No 'I do'.
Idolatry. Yes,

her father felt grim
but, in war, the fleet comes first.
To leave port safely

they must pray, must pay,
must give away some dear thing.
The unseen goddess

loves the iron smell,
loves bribes, smoke. So they say.
His blood. Hers. Her breath

rattling in the masts,
blood shimmer of ore flushing
round the keels. Blade. Skin.

Iphianassa
splattering down the altar.
War boats on water.

There, Mem.
                You see how
such blind faith can lead a king
to kill his daughter?

Jackdaws

Some days we try to close our ears
like this morning when we wake to hear
jackdaws squawking in the disused chimney
where the hand of the gale has thrown them,
their cries unnerved and unnerving,
a scuffling amplified in our skulls,
as though we can hear the heart of the house
beating against brick.

We leave for work telling ourselves
the birds will find their own way out,
that we're late already. In any case,
we're only renting, can change nothing.

In the car, the crying yammers in our heads
so, halfway down the flooded lane,
we reverse, and home again, fetch the hammer,
claw off the board that blocks the flue,
let fall the sooty mess of nests
and windwashed gravel, force up
the glossed-in sash, then wait.

The wary birds stay hidden,
quiet as our held breath.

Eventually three jackdaws squinny out,
a slow flap of feathers scattering ash,
brightening again into their own blackness,
as each bird senses the open sash, the upthrust
of light and wind welcoming their wings.

This time it's easy, wiping away droppings,
knocking hardboard tight in the chimney gap.

But there are other days when we close our ears
look away, don't drive back.

Then through the window crack, we'll hear
a squabble of jackdaws cawing –
What have you done? What have you left undone?

Aliens

In the summer that my granny's mouth went strange,
her tongue sideways, frustrating her lips,
her words a scrawl of pencil on a pad,
my mother was always driving,
taut as a string pulled between two posts,
her hands sharp on the sandwich bread,
slapping thick doorsteps onto formica,
reversing in at midnight,
and up early in a clatter of angry pans.
One night when it was morning already,
she'd sat thinking of her mother's life,
her hand held tight watching her,
and then driven back in a low gear,
winding through the village where she was born
and up high through trees, tired
by her imaginings of an empty bed
with clean white sheets.
As her car climbed dark boughed bends
lighting garlic, startling deer,
and the valley fell away beneath,
the sky grew larger, and she saw
a ring of faces in the air
looking down at the hill, the beeches,
looking down at her.

My father talked of night-manoeuvres,
but my mother shook her head,
not helicopters, not planes, but faces
that formed a face she never saw again.

In the Lane

We are speaking of the killing of children,
and I'm waiting for her to say,
'the world's gone bad,'
wanting a comfortable reply,
wanting to see her with her sisters
in an old-fashioned pose, pinafore on,
feet slipping in the safe sunny lane
between the wars, *poor but happy.*
Instead, she says, 'Something I've never told...'
how walking back from school
in an untidy knot of children,
she'd raised her head
to an oak, the ivy twisting round the trunk,
the big tree shadowing and dappling
the lane's limestone walls. She'd raised
her head to laugh and seen the man
perched high. He had them in his sights.
She saw his finger tightening on the gun.
My seven-year-old mother
couldn't run or scream
or nudge the others, but stood
as if the coldest stillest girl on earth.
Someone shouted,
'A lorry's coming. Move!'
The children fell into the gateway of a field.
When she looked up, her pinafore was smeared
with mud and sand, a reason for her tears.

And through these last months,
I push her home along the lane, thinking
how none of this might ever have happened.

Birth

A story children love to hear
but can never remember.
'She was born on'…a biographer's note
that says nothing of the day in December
your sixteen-year-old mother and your father
struggle with the cold,
stopping the gaps in the plaster
with his granny's torn petticoat,
laying scarves and old socks
against the undercracks of doors,
lighting the gas which seeps
into running flames along each wall.

When you come slithering out,
they name you Myrtle
for the cottage which leaks fire and rain
while your mother sluices
herself down with water from the china jug
and your father fills his pipe
and worries and coughs
thinking how he really is a man
now he has a child. But you can't remember
any of it: Old Daise, your mother's stepmother,
embarrassing your mother
with a Romany blessing
and some eggs from the goose.

Before the six other children,
before the sixty-a-day Senior Service,
before the horses,
there is just you and them, and, after the rain,
winter sun whitens the old man's beard
which loops from beech to yew to beech
tracing the whole steep hill, and there is
your mother, bloody, and singing
with her long hair down,
the way you always wanted to remember.

Haiku from Lucretius

II *Wind and Water*

> *The hidden atoms of the wind flow like water and, like water,*
> *churn out maelstroms.*
>
> (DRN BOOK 1 *ll.* 265-97)

Mem, you've watched a gale
whip up wave clutter, capsize
ships, blow away clouds?

A racing twister
rip out trees, juggle them, then
scatter them on plains,

batter mountain peaks
with forestsplintering blasts?
Heard unseen thunder?

You have seen runnels
swell into torrents brimming
with icemelt, swirling

uprooted orchards
to the river's mouth, whirling
arms of trees down weirs.

Bridges won't withstand
the skeltering storm water.
So a burn swollen

by deluging rain
drives its force against arches,
smashes heavy stone,

hurls away and drowns
whatever resists the flow
of its wild currents.

Whirl wind or whirl pool,
both smash, twirl, rip, wind things up
in sucking eddies.

So, wind must be made
of invisible bodies,
since, in its effects,

it is like water,
whose visible bodies – burns
rivers, vortices,

canals, springs and seas –
are moving and substantial
to your naked eye.

The Shirt

(for Coen Wessel)

As we're born thirsty,
in a breaking sac of water,
which splits and spills,
reforming in cloud spray,
springs and ditches,
so, Coen, let's say this shirt
is made of water, and that we put it on
whenever we swim in woodland lakes,
with rushes pulling at our legs,
and smell that twiggy effervescence
on our skin.
    A shirt of water can be
mud brown, or striped by navy and sky,
turquoise patterned by sunfish and weeds,
patched by dark shapes,
a geography of underwater boulders
that cools its cloth as we pass over
or warms us in the lull of sand bars.
    Whatever fabric water mimics,
it always fits us, growing with our arms
and chest, stretching round our crawl
or breast stroke.
        In this shirt, with its fluid seams,
we'll swim up mountain rivers
as they zigzag downwards.
We'll leap and fly up waterfalls.
We'll pull round headlands
against the current of a spring tide.
When coastguards shake their heads and sigh,
we'll swim back towards the town
where, somewhen earlier, the running
of feet and the calling of sirens
echoed in the lanes, streets, squares,
and the yellowcoated fishermen
will haul us in,
thinking we own a magic caul.
They'll nod and murmur, 'lucky, lucky',
and offer us rough towels and tea
from flasks. Though they rub us dry
in the fishy air,
they won't see the shirt

that has thinned to a mist,
the shirt we'll still be wearing
that made us believe, with each stroke,
we could live.

Madron Well

Rag well: a source of water supposed to be of miraculous origin or to have supernatural healing powers.

We've read about it so we follow
the unmarked path between hazels,
longing to get out of the close valley
to the saltiness of sea air.
'Is this it?' we ask, staring at mud.
But at the second pool,
the rustle of rags startles us:
slither of Liberty silk, a linen sleeve,
shredded silver foil, a chiffon scarf,
a school sock ringed with sweat,
bra straps, denim, unravelled wool, belts, ties.

What makes this holy is not the seep
of water in the muddy grass, but the vision
of a business man running from the layby
where he's parked his Porsche,
slipping off his jacket,
tearing a sleeve from his shirt,
the schoolboy removing his sock, limping home
his left foot rubbing inside his trainer,
the young mother unhooking her bra
leaking milk into her cotton dress,
and the others who makes wishes for others
cutting string vests, old knickers,
handkerchiefs with stitched initials,
the stretching up of their tensed bodies,
their fingers knotting relics to the hazel,
praying that no one sees them do it,
then praying for a cure.

Fireclay

First you strip to the waist,
then you pull off the lid,
dip in your hands.

I like the way you scoop
the clay on finger ends.
I like the thick whitecreaminess of clay.

I like your bare back and chest
that I have kissed and touched.
I cannot speak to you.

You step into the chimney.
You take the clay and start
to mould it on the brushed surface
of the bricks. You're eager
to patch the crack,
make another skin.

My dark man, with the pale skin,
soon you will be darkened by soot,
whitened by clay.

And later, out of the fireplace,
all your coolness will burn against me,
while the clay dries,
and the fire goes on escaping through the crack.

Dialect

You say the children beat it out of you,
the Donegal rhythm, the immigrant words.

When you sing, your pitch is perfect,
but when you speak, you are untrue.

You tell how once, in Austria, you waded through snow
to pick the last bright apple from a black tree.

When I bite the skin,
your fictions are cidery on my tongue.

Where do voices go?

They're buried in your chest, your lungs,
return when you lie dying.

Your voice still tastes of bitter, of big-leafed tobacco-burning smoke.

You say it was a dream,
but it's amber, hardened by my body's memory.

Mrs Rochester

When he's sent Grace away, he likes
to snuff the candle with his fingers,
wave away the burning wax smell of it
a priest in this dark musty church.

He lies down with me on the mattress
he heaved up here alone. At first,
he came for sleep but now he undresses my breasts,
fingering my nipples, gasping, making me gasp.

I have draped the roof-room in leftover white lace,
big fancy swathes of it. I am his virgin,
just like the games we used to play.
When he pushes in, he calls out 'Jane, Jane'
missing her. If I could bleed for him,
I would. I'll rub against him later,
when he sleeps, to get my pleasure.
Whose name shall I call?

The morning after, like a good wife, I'll watch him
from the attic window, riding out,
relieved, the spark back in his eye.

And there are nights
when I study him, light every line
of his face with the candle. He'll wake
terrified at my big trembling shadow.
'What do you want?' he'll cry.
His terror angers me. All I want to do
is light his face with the flame.
He holds my arms, fights me,
pushing me back upstairs.

But in the waxy darkness,
when I bite him, or tear his hair,
he calls out, 'again, again'.

Outdoor Wedding in Vermont

Waiters sauté over small fires, trick
delicacies out of the dark, balance

them among pyramids of flowers.
The groom's speech. How he loves his best man.

How the Barbie bride is homely but she'll do.
Bottled laughter. Good mannered, they leave

on the dot of midnight. Fairytale rules.
Later the wife will wrinkle off her gloves

while raccoons come out of the woods
through the sickle leaves of sweet chestnut

stepping over spiked half-opened shells
to eat canapés in their clawed hands.

The Nag's Head

One night our men wore brooches,
shaded their eyes, reddened their lips.
The paste and french silver shone
like armour in the pub, where we
played pool. We told the locals
we were a club. Youths eyed us
envious of all the rubies,
sapphires, emeralds faking it
in the smoke of The Nag's Head.
We'd eaten quails' eggs, drunk port,
but it wasn't enough. Our men
went on display like peacocks,
and we were the hens, protecting
them. Their eyes glittered
as they took aim, and, in the gloom,
the diamonds were tiny flames,
burning slow, retreating,
advancing again.

National Trust Membership

Out in the mists of the meadow,
there's a huge glasshouse, its panes
nuzzled by veined escaping figs.

Grapes hang from the lintel,
brush my head. Did I mention that I'm naked
and looking for you?

That I grind
my feet on granite chips,
on sand, on slivers of earthenware?

I've never shouted under glass before,
and when I do, the fibrous growth and humid air
soak up the sound of your name.

I'm sweating. Where are you?
Hiding under a canopy of hemp,
or sluicing your legs

with cold fast water from the big tap?
When I catch you,
we'll lie down on small seeds of gravel.

We'll lie under slatted shelves,
glimpse sturdy shoes, woollen ankles,
and hear murmurings, the ritual naming of plants.

Back at the Dry

he hopes he'll laugh with his mates
about the voice of the tommy-bouncer
asking for food in the dripping shaft,

and how he thought he'd heard the sea
washing towards him in the wheal,
yet followed his spirit anyway,

hoping it would lead him to a seam
of cassiterite that would change everything.
He'll laugh about the sandwich he left

on the ledge, the lunch he'd needed
when he hit the lode and didn't want to leave.
His grandfathers too had wanted more bread

as they ate in darkness, saving on candlewax.
But the tommy-bouncers took
that extra crust, their scrabbling hands

twitched it from the kibble, before the men had even set
their dets. In return, the whistling spirits
buoyed them, their whispers singing,

'Mine yourself like a lode, trim your wick,
and, we, the tommy-bouncers, will sit with you,
and save you from a land-slip.'

Back at the dry, he showers off the ore
with Fairy soap, jokes, just as he'd hoped,
about his number nearly being up, then

pushes open those double doors
on to the Atlantic, where the red stream
washes round the cliffs to the town.

He hears again watery songs, scufflings,
breaths that blew him up the shaft
until he rose like a gull on air.

Ponte Sant'Angelo, Rome

The river remembers the unwrapping
of angels, when their hands first offered
whip, thorn or plank, and smiles carved their faces.
The river knows the handbag sellers too.
They dance to iPods and sleep on its banks.
The river hears the Finanza's engines
revving and ticking on the avenue's side.
Some days the river fears it is losing
its flow, like Bernini's smiling maniacs,
mind meandering to Caesar, barges,
its job as the city's extinguisher,
the votive carnations thrown into eddies,
torn heads bobbing away in the current.
Propitiation – it tries that old word
on its rushing tongues, but tributaries
garble the sound to a *susurration*.
All the river can do is moan and lap,
swaying the tourist boats in its cupped hands.
Some nights its weeping roars a lullaby
into the ears of its lodgers, cools them
and their sleeping bags, with its thinnest spray,
then streams into those dreams of a village,
where children walk miles to find a river.

Irrigator in the Far Field

I look away, but it draws my eye.
The water inside me wants it.
My hand wants to write it.
It's like

a cossack's whirling legs,
gauzy nets hung out to dry,
a Roman fountain pumping
zigzags of spectra
that cross and flail and cross
and linger in an afterlife,
arcs of falling glass
that splinter on furrows.

It's a set of muslin flags
semaphoring
the melting of ice-caps,
the flooding of valleys
where packed children
watch water settle,
and look for ripples
that show their old road home.

I try to write microcosms:
drops on slate like cool balls of mercury,
the pool in a lupin leaf.

But the faucet's jammed.
The irrigator twizzles, forcing its thin veils
up through a waste of English rain.

Send and Receive

You see mountains, blue, distant, on the ground.
You see the city lurch at you through air:
I'm safe. There was no bomb. The delayed plane
is tracking down the sky. At home she's found
the e-mail. Misses you again. Touch is rare.
Electric codes and chatter mask the pain.
I'm all right: CUT. These words may be for show.
DRAFT: *when she was my daughter's age, they'd moored*
this small girl's father to a log and kicked
him down the river in the floods. They know
the acts of blood. Your camera records
her face, the antelopes on her frock. She picked
one man out in a police parade. He was a friend.
DELETE: photos and words you cannot send.

Delete these words you're not allowed to send...
DRAFT:...*on the lake in my neighbour's canoe.*
The shrimps were delicious. The fish was good.
Your fingers linger on ATTACH. Hit SEND:
Pixels are not enough, blurred shots too few.
You cannot tell her everything you should.
The plane was banking down towards us,
and we ran. HIDE: *a foot wrapped in a rag.*
She's sold her maize to buy his ARVs:
CUT: *if she's tested, she won't make a fuss.*
Her brother says there's money in a bag.
Hallucinating? Young enough to tease?
Tonight you log on. Log off. Don't tell.
The e-mail's silent in your head. Just as well.

Her e-mail. Silence in your head. Just as well
you bought that silver from the jeweller
down the road. Handmade present for your daughter.
Prices here are nothing. If she ever wants to sell...
There's not enough ice in the cooler
to soothe her fever, not enough water
to wash her brother's legs, not enough hands
to hold the smallest baby. Offer a lift
to that teacher hiking to the border.
Somehow, he trusts you. Tells how he lands
odd jobs at night, how the shared room's a gift
as long as he works twelve hours to order.
You drop him in darkness. Bribes make no sound.
Once through the checkpoint, he doesn't turn round.

Once through the forest, you don't turn around.
You're climbing high, zooming in from trees,
to spaces where children search for wood to keep.
Your driver takes you out to the urban pound
to tread on corrugated doors that need no keys.
You're photographing eyes too stunned to weep.
You're visiting a village without parents.
You send: *the virus spreads but people cope.*
DELETE: *those helpful hands and grieving faces.*
Bulldozers are roaring towards the tents
which served as houses, seemed to offer hope
before the voting ate away the neighbours' graces
before the suffering spies named a friend
as enemy and an enemy as friend.

An enemy? These boys want to be your friends,
hoping your photographs will bring them money.
But you're trying to shake off that last brother
who bargains with party cards, asks you to lend
your camera as a witness. *Look at this sunny
country. See the rose farm where our mother
grafted before she died.* Tonight. Some reception
with canapés and champagne on the hoof.
Imagine your eye's a shutter or the sun.
Sees only this moment. No exceptions.
Be smooth, not disapproving, or aloof.
Small talk. You'll need to stick it out, not run.
The host's absent. It's a secret. In a cell?
There's shame about his sickness. Please don't tell.

There's shame about the sickness. Please don't tell
her that you *pandered to a murderer:*
CUT. Yesterday, you stood and listened
to the president's ranting. No one could quell
his paranoia. Tried to think of ways to further her
treatment. *Hear me...* But you were threatened.
Silence then. Edit the story. *Leeches,
apparently virgins too, will kill
the virus.* Tried to report but the system's down.
The letters float and tangle through long speeches.
Outside some actors set up posters, still
the crowd with rhythmic voices. A clown
lion-masked, shows how the virus dances:
from body to body, the predator prances.

From body to body, the predator prances
stabbing his claws into the impala,
buckling knuckled knees on the savanna.
Draft: *there are still roses. Perhaps advances*
in medicine. Blue lined mountains. Galas,
where the boss deals out food like manna
to the workers under a roof of sheets.
There are the girls, heads loaded, carrying grain,
carrying babies, lending parents their arms.
There are not enough votes to change the streets.
There are not enough drugs to deal with the pain.
There are not enough voices to raise the alarm.
You're typing late. *Antiques and silver.*
The rich are revving engines. Quick! Shiver.

The rich are revving engines. Quick shiver
of moth wings brushing skin on the veranda
flittering over the blue pool at night.
The gardener's at his daughter's, by the river.
He'd collapsed behind the jacaranda.
He could have died here. Took himself out of sight.
To the daughter he scarcely knew. Sent cash.
She has the bed prepared, guesses by her sweats
and sore limbs that he's passed the virus on
through his need or love. He was always rash.
She scoops the water in her hands, and wets
his head. Thinks maybe baptism is a con.
For him, she's left the factory. Clicks her tongue.
Her voice floats into a lengthening hum.

The sound floats into a lengthening hum.
Someone's fixed the system. Needed clearance.
Took all day. News is flying now. Sweeping
out of in-trays. *A predator has come.*
People trail, drawn to the appearance
of the singing actors, their mad leaping,
notes seeping into ears still undeafened:
CUT. Switch off. Take a trip to the mountains.
Cranes flap purple wings, wag their golden crowns.
Sunsets flare. Dazzle. This could be heaven.
Small children wash under the hose's fountain.
A lion is coming. Finds his prey and frowns.
Buffalo run over the warm expanses.
The predator leaps. Camouflaged. Lances.

The predator leaps. Camouflaged glances
hurt, imagined words hurt. The unopened e-mails
tell a story. Maybe she's not waiting after all.
Without you, maybe, her new self dances?
Draft: *you could come over…* Sound of nails
hammered into posts. Builders making walls.
DELETE: *this girl fits a condom on a bottle.*
The men are drinking beer. **Wouldn't use it.**
She flaunts herself and they anticipate.
You want love? *she says, flirting at full throttle.*
Yes. They want it. Want her to slide over, sit
on laps, give them some lip. Before it's too late.
You like me? *She's got them all a quiver.*
I'm HIV. *She makes the condom slither.*

I'm HIV. She makes the condom slither
down the bottle. *You could die, if you sleep*
with me. They walk away, ashamed, surprised.
Every night since, she's used her come hither
looks to attract them. Since those steep
bills came in for drugs, since she's mired
in debt, this is one way to pay, and pay back
the bank, the boss, the chemist and the school.
She has not hands enough to hold her brothers.
She has not hands enough to use their tools.
She has not strength enough to mend the crack
left in the wall by her father's drill. Covers
her ears when the state wreckers come. That thrum
reminds her how he worked before he fell numb.

Remind her how it worked? Before he went dumb
and didn't reply to her news: oh, press delete.
Empty the trash bin. That story he'd told her.
She knew when he went there, there'd be some
girl he'd fall for. Distance just breeds deceit.
She should have come. Should have been bolder.
At thirty-five, we're in our prime, aren't we?
You try: *each line from now on stands for a year.*
You press: SEND. *Stats:* prime numbers appear.
That girl gets a year. Year with her child. The queue
at the clinic gives her answers and tears.
Year with a parent, year without fears.
She carries her child there, all wrapped around,
before the predator can bring them to ground.

Before the predator brings her to ground,
she'll try to buy a party card, make it known
that she's in line for drugs. Her father
– she'll bury. Her nephew's song is the sound
that will serve as a choir. The bank wants her loan
repaid fast. She dips her arms in a lather
of soap and bandages, old cotton dresses.
Patterns can still distract her. Those deer prints,
ochre on crimson, that zigzag batik,
that red wrap for his legs, the sponge she presses
on his arms, long and small, the tiny splint
that strengthens his calf...if only he'd speak...
open his long-lashed eyes, move his head's soft down.
Don't let the predator bring him to ground.

Don't let the predator bring her to ground,
you murmur as your camera flashes.
Each line's a year. Thirty-five's average.
How will you live if the virus is found?
How do you feel when your system crashes?
When you're still grieving, what can you salvage?
Her cousin's mother-in-law takes them in
once their home lies shattered on the street.
She holds the children by each hand and whirls
them, till their legs go flying in a spin,
and they're screaming, shouting, as their feet
catherine-wheel, chair-o-plane in air, swirl,
kaleidoscope and kick. Glad, lovely sound,
as they cry with laughter on the ground.

As they cry with laughter on the ground...
delete these words you find so hard to send?
Your e-mails grow silent. You know too well
how at the checkpoint, he won't turn around,
that touch turns friend to enemy to friend.
Despite the shame about the sickness, you'll tell.
Body to body. The predator prances.
The quick are revving engines. The rich shiver,
as voices float into a lengthening hum.
A predator leaps through camouflaged glances.
Aching eyes see a wrinkled girl slither
out on to the bed. A fresh line, new sum.
When her crying screams out, shaking the ground,
you long for the mountains to echo her sound.

Aid Worker

Back from another continent,
he'll seek out fresh quail's eggs,
their speckles freckling in tiny egg boxes.
He'll hammer steak to a thin slither,
tenderised and bloody.
He gives her her first taste
of mussels from a big iron pot on the dusty floor,
the purple shells unhinging in the heat.
He tears the bread and hands it to her,
dips his crust into the garlicky wine.
He tells her nothing she would like to know,
only that tomorrow, he'll buy coriander, hot basil,
baby eggplants, an armful of oranges and limes.
On these nights, inside the small walls
of the English city,
                    he'll eat himself away
from Africa, and then slowly,
                    when the hunger returns,
he'll gnaw his way back.

The Phone Tower Wood

Out from under the phone towers, on quiet hooves,
    deer munch stems of Queen of the Night
before the tall, greening buds
    can ever uncup
their veined dusty crimson light,
    their pools of blood-black bruises.

It's a strange consolation to say, over and over,
    on the phone, or in pubs to city friends,
the deer have eaten the tulips again.
    On a rare evening, I'll see all three of them
cantering over the tussocky field,
    back to the phone tower trees and their humming cover.

Laburnum

looks benign
like that girl in a green dress,
hurrying along the edge
of The Avenue and The Drive,
yellow hair tossed by wind.

Suburban laburnum,
the sound of ease.

You want it, though
farmers chop through
its dark heart,
and parents lop it
from their hedges,
knowing every root
and seed can kill.

But ask yourself
who planted
these three trees,
over the brown river
beside the fields,
their yellow chains
trailing among alders,
their pods floating
past farmyards,
past playgrounds
and under private bridges,
spiked and gated.

Some day you'll walk with Midas
long riverbanks, all turned yellow,
where you can't see brown water
for reflected, mesmeric gold.

The Resurrection Plant

When I've lifted it from its box
and inspected its shrunken head,

then I stroke my gift, a snatch
of tumbleweed that blew

through the prospectors' empty town,
bouncing along a dried up river.

I watch it grow expansive
in the bowl of shallow water,

and whisper, who are you? It whispers back,
a fist of dust, a fern, a little forest.

The wind scooped me from everglades,
hurled me across the night ice of deserts.

My spores are the sulphurous spark
of fireworks. Give me the sun,

and I'll give it back to you
in the open flower of burning coals.

But for now I'm a parched tongue
that must suck on your water.

As the bowl dries out, I watch
hygroscopic fingers curl back into a hand,

a fist, a head, talismanic, shrunken
that turns on me and says:

now, what are you?

The Stove

(after Pollock's practice and Cézanne's painting)

At dawn, he huffs the screws of paper
to a flickering blue, slams

glass doors to keep the sparks in,
edges past canvases that patch the floor.

Each morning, heat rises to the gap
between the cross beams.

Night after night, in that big red barn,
the embers cool.

The log pile, with its double rime
of snow and bark, diminishes.

When his wife asks him why
he lights the stove,

burning up his orchard and the birch
felled two years before the frozen winter,

he'll say, 'This could be the day
I start to work again.'

Reflux: The Japanese Bridge at Giverny

For years you quell water-weeds,
struggle with the sun,
strive for clouds in your water-trap,

letting the fall of water, the floating Os
catch light and wind between their gaps.
But the watched for clouds seep in,

fogging agapanthus, irises.
You walk the garden in a mist,
guessing that woman is Blanche,

guessing she's picking caterpillars
from nasturtiums, though you know
they'll be stripped,

the orange faces shredded.
The wisteria's a crude tangle of ropes.
The lilies are smeared white-gold.

You shout, 'I call this yellow.
What do you call it?'
Amnesia of colour.

You're forced to squint,
reading *sienna* (intermittent
bleeding) *red*,

cobalt (drowning)
blue, painting by word
in a torture of monochrome.

And after the knife,
the waiting,
head sandbagged,

no sudden moves,
month after month of black flecks
in your sights, until

the new glasses from Germany,
and the bridge suddenly burning
trees and earth together,

a hell on water,
raging in ochre, in orange,
demanding you.

The Trip to Monterey
(i.m. Imogen Rizq)

You drive over the river
the Mexicans wade nightly.

You're wearing a straw hat for protection,
shell earrings, a sea-coloured silk shirt.

You've lined your eyes with kohl
that you bought in Tunis,

made a picnic, white rolls, cheese,
bottled water. Bangles slide down your arm.

I'm guessing images that were true
in other places. Knowing what happened,

I've never asked what happened.
Instead I remember you leaving Walton Street,

the egg you refused to waste,
propping it between drawings,

driving it home, cross-country,
in the hired van. Your tenderness for things:

I remember you saying goodbye
to an antique infuser

dangling its perforated silver
back into its box. You hated

to break a plate, stain a cup.
And you'd been across oceans,

safely, waving your wild eastern hands.
I cannot imagine the road from Brownsville,

the old drunk careering in his car.
I cannot imagine the burning of you,

flesh and bone.
What I can see is the egg,

rolling from your mother's table,
the blood-spot quivering on the imagined floor.

Trevail

You won't remember
how we fetched the mortice
from the farm, big as a castle key
and how it wouldn't work at first
and how the cottage was forbidden.

You won't remember
the small cotton shirt
my mother gave you
and how I ran rainwater
into the stone sink of the spence,
washing the blue cotton in water so soft
the suds wouldn't rinse
but dripped on dry marram and plantain.

You won't remember the cornflowers
I bought in Nancledra,
easily slotting the money through
the slit of the black metal box.

You won't remember their ragged blueness,
how they shone a blue light in the brown jug
as if we'd torn fragments out of the sky
and put pieces of air in the dark room.

You won't remember that I left you one evening,
climbed down through the lichen jungle,
ran down to River Cove on the river path
and watched seals, slick black commas
rolling in the waves, noses surfing,
surfacing on rocks.

You won't ever know or remember
the giddy pull of the seals basking
or the way I could have waded out
to meet them, nose to nose.

You won't remember my return
through the gate of the bouldered garden

or how I saw the blue shirt blowing,
dry and aired, tugging
at the hills of Wicca and Trevail.

You won't ever remember how
the small blue shape of your shirt
brought me back.

Ferries at Southsea

At George's, we see the ferries coming in,
huge trays of light buoyant in the dark blue evening,
floating out of the night towards the palm trees,
towards the young drunk spraycanning the pavement,
his words sputtering away. We watch the ferries,
coming in, their unsteady flickerings like poems,
freighted with the dead, the living and the refugees,
carrying those who don't mind the long way over,
lotus-eaters or dreamers or souls returning,
lit up and floating, like lights themselves,
like the strings of lights that curve and stretch
along Clarence Parade, lighting us to our cars
when we leave at midnight. Soon those night-travellers
will disembark too, dragging their rucksacks
down slipways, smuggling their talents through customs,
dreaming firm ground under their feet,
dreaming, as they try to enter a new berth,
of their children in safe houses
in quiet streets where nights can be dull,
and the only flash is the flash of a car's light
on the elder flowers, crowded and sultry.

Bulb Primer

'I have just learnt to love a hyacinth.'
'And how might you learn? By accident or argument?'
JANE AUSTEN: Northanger Abbey

Protect yourself. Wear gloves.
Touching the skin may raise
yours to an itchy flush.

Wrap in brown paper.
Hide in your blackest place. Keep cool,
but not too cold. Forget.

When days and roots
are lengthening, remove
from the mock night.

Set the blanched shoot
on a forcing glass
in a north light.

Watch white roots
string into water.
Watch greening beaks

become green tongues,
juiced fingers unclutching
a fat stem, the leaf stores

of fleshy opening stars.
Learn to love, not the scent
that tracks you round the house,

but the balancing in air
of an underground bud.
When it's all over,

plunge into quiet earth
and know, each year,
you'll want again

this likeness you've made
of something wrapped and hidden,
some secret grown in the dark.

Haiku from Lucretius
III *The Sensuous Proof of Atomism*
(DRN BOOK 1 *ll*. 298-0328)

You can't see a voice,
but you hear airwaves vibrate.
You know heat through touch.

Clothes dampen, hung out
on a wave-breaking beach, dry
on an inland bush.

Do you see mizzle
creeping into the cloth's weave?
Can you watch it leave?

A ring wears away.
You do not see the gold go,
thinning day by day.

Drips bore holes in stone.
Under the earth, a rubbed flint
strikes atoms from the plough's blade.

Passeggiata.
Who sees the step's curve deepen
under the crowd's feet?

Tourists shake the hands
of bronze statues by the gate.
A joke that wears thin.

We do not see salt
eating away the chalk cliffs
until the house falls.

Our eyes don't freeze frame,
can't attenborough a vine's
snaking growth through trees.

We are not brahmins,
don't brush away ants, fearing
to crush the unseen.

We need a glass lens,
not our eyes. Then we'll admit
the hidden matter.

Notes for a poem

If I want to write
>about white willowseed floating in green air,
and I really mean
>my mother in a red wheelchair, borrowed from the Red Cross,
and I really mean,
>the memory of my mother, a second-hand memory,
because they told me – I wasn't there –
>'we pushed her right up here',
in the face of ruts, flints,
>and hardcore hidden under the mud of the bridleway
or whatever name the map gives to this track,
>and instead, I write of the laminae of green leaves,
of beech, hazel, elder, sycamore,
>and look for far-fetched words, like *green earth of Verona,*
viridescent, fern-green, viridian,
>and really mean the bottle-green
without the glaze of glass,
>and the brambles, a tangled mess from apex to ground
and back again,
>that is a wood in summer, with its green mat of sound,
its flashes and ovals
>of sun wavering through the leaves' filter,
how, then, will I be writing of my mother
>and the way we miss her,
by writing about the white willowseed,
>floating through the green air in May
two years after she was here
>jolting over the rutted mud of lime and clay
breathless among
>the photosynthesising trees?

All my notes repeat
>repeat   repeat,   more or less, this:

willowseed drifting through unabsorbed green
a white speck floating in the corner of the eye
or in the corner of the mind's eye
suspended yet moving quietly
among the layers of oxygenating leaves

Sussex Road at Night in December

There's a house flexed with lights
which a man's fixed to his eaves
in a cold wind signalling snow.

He's woven the hedge with bulbs,
his warm rendering of frost.
The icicles drip, on, off, on.

There's the lit outline of the house,
the chimney, the roof, the walls,
flat and upright,

like a door to the Downs
whose dark back
I see resting inside.

I'm going in, past the owl
on the road's reflector,
past the badger's pelt on the verge,

into the night view where three deer
canter in a field that will be
frost strewn by morning.

I'm running up
those loose shoulders of chalk,
untangling the moon from the oak

where it's caught, a sliver
split by the phone wire,
like the cracked voice of a friend's trouble.

I'm climbing out,
with the moon in my hands,
healed to a full round,

and I'm wiring it over the door
like the porch light that clicks on
from the real house I go back to.

Waggoner's Wells

you tell me they're not wells
and they're not hammer ponds
as there's no iron and no one
knows who widened the river
or why they made these pools
lead into one another trailing
down to a marsh of agrimony
watermint the dying spears of flags
harbouring coots' nests

close up you can't see the big fish
only the occasional slow bubbling
from the twenty-seven pound carp
caught here at breakfast which the boy
threw back with a splash as loud as
that labrador pup bellyflopping in
after a stick a duck a fish
rising from the sandbed
to the breaking surface scum
where the white moulted feathers
their soft curves moored
on their own reflections
are not tiny canoes
and the smoke of gnats
is not smoke is not mimicking
the tumbling swarm of minnows
in the glaucous green-gold water
forming and reforming like birds
when they are dots or streaks
which shoal and telescope and fan
through a cold sky

the wind moving the sun
on the pools and rippling
the oakbark and underside of leaves
with restless water marks
is not an intended mirroring
of woodgrain on a balked trunk
and though we seem to be just
eating our picnic from the Tesco bag
we're joining up slow bubbles
to big rings assuming fish
seeing our own heads
in water through foreshortened trees

until you say, 'look, the nettles are breathing'
as the dust floats off them into the air
and the dust is not breath
and the skeins of water
where the stream clears
are not skeins but fast-flowing
shallows connecting pool
to weir to marsh to pool
silting and flooding currencies
improbable assumptions

Calling from the Hidden River

Worrying that you'll go while we're away,
I call you from Heddon's Mouth, holding the phone
to the Heddon as it runs under the big
cool eggs of blue and mauve rocks, hoping
you'll hear the hidden river bubbling below us
under granite, its fresh water seeping to salt.
I want you to hear the voice of the world's spring
in the crass cackle of geese guarding a hotel
and the crash of the waves booming in caves
on Wild Pear beach. High on the coastal path,
I wish the phone would carry the scent of gorse
and the long view of the village in the valley's crease,
stretching miles down its one street to the sea.
I wish you could sense, before we're cut off,
the white uplift of gulls on blue thermals
or the gush of rivers crossing at Watersmeet.
By Watermouth Cove, standing in a field of rabbits,
the sound fading, I wish all this into our call:
the clanking of pale masts, last year's ferns
brightening to copper, ripples firing
keels with light grainy ghosts, the sweet crush
of bluebells on the grass near the watchtower,
but best of all, as the signal wavers, then holds,
your voice, hoarse, and shouting, *I'm still here*.

NOTES

Haiku versions of Lucretius *(pages 34, 40, 72)*

De Rerum Natura is a didactic hexameter poem. Choosing haiku for these translated versions from Book I may seem odd, but Lucretius' close eye on nature means there are several haiku moments of intense economical vision in the original, e.g. 'stilicidi casus lapidem cavat' or 'fluctifrago suspensae in litore vestes/uvescunt'. The haiku form seems to serve the inflected nature of Latin too. Lucretius addressed his argument for the material atomic nature of the world to Memmius; I have changed Memmius to Mem to suggest a more contemporary relationship. Sometimes I have transferred significances associatively, e.g. the reference to Hymen in 'Aulis' becomes a distorted wedding scene, 'hymns, his men' and so on. Iphianassa is usually known as Iphigenia. I have kept Iphianassa for the sound and to defamiliarise the story of Agamemnon's sacrifice of his daughter.

Back at the Dry *(page 51)*

Thanks to Ian Davey of Geevor Tin Mine for an informative tour.

'The dry': the tin miners' locker room.

'Tommy-bouncers': the spirits of the mine, often appeased with food.

'Dets': detonators.